This book belongs to:
_____

For the sweetest fruit of all, Teddy x

Dita Von Teese quote printed with the owner's full permission.

Characters and events in this book are fictitious.
Any reference contained in this book to public figures and their works
does not constitute or imply their endorsement or recommendation.

Copyright © 2020 Michaela Skilney

All rights reserved. No part of this book may be reproduced in any form
or used in any manner without permission in writing from the copyright
owner, except for the use of brief quotations in a book review.

ISBN 978-0-6489196-1-2 (Paperback Edition)
ISBN 978-0-6489196-0-5 (Hardback Edition)

Written by Michaela Skilney
Illustrated by Vikki Chiu

Printed and distributed by IngramSpark
First edition printed October 2020

Published by Michaela Skilney
Victoria, Australia

For orders, permission requests and all other enquiries, please visit:
www.michaelaskilney.com

JUST PEACHY
By Michaela Skilney

Illustrated by Vikki Chiu

"You can be the ripest, juiciest peach in the world,
and there's still going to be somebody
who doesn't like peaches."

- Dita Von Teese

Dita ballerina was a peach who loved to dance. She'd practise and perfect her moves whenever she had the chance.

She could do the Macarena and perform an arabesque.

She could do a cheeky fan dance like the starlets of burlesque.

Nothing made her happier than performing in her room.

Never had a stone fruit danced with so much vavavoom!

One day a travelling dance troupe sashayed into town, led by none other than Ms Von Teese - a dancer world renowned.

"I'm looking for 'the next big thing', a dancer with pizzazz. A fruit who loves to dance along to hip hop, pop and jazz."

So the very next day, when evening fell, she planned to audition. Dancing alongside Ms Von Teese was Dita's number one mission!

Dita went, with mum in tow, to show what she could do.
"I cannot wait to be a star," she said to her mum. "Can you?"

"Don't be disappointed if she's not on the same page,
if a ripe and juicy peach isn't what she wants for her stage."

"Don't be silly," Dita said, while hugging her mother tight.
"How could I fail to 'wow' her if I give it all my might?"

"Peaches aren't for everyone," she said with a comforting tone.
"Just remember, the most important opinion of you is your very own."

In the middle of the front row Ms Von Teese took her position, amongst a sea of flowers - given to persuade her decision.

"Dita!" she called, from a list of names.
"Little peach, it's your go."

So Dita leapt into the air …

… and landed on one toe!

She tapped and twirled and shimmied about,
with top hat in hand.

Every triumphant flip she did, on her feet she'd land.

But Ms Von Teese,
the greatest burlesque dancer of them all,
didn't find Dita's dance routine exceptional at all.

"I've seen enough," she said to Dita.
"It's time, little peach, to leave."
But the little ballerina peach had one last move up her sleeve.

Surely she'd impress with what her peach fuzz could do.

She rubbed her hands on her hips and sides and out sprung a ballet tutu!

She performed a pirouette. Her technique was by the book.

But still, despite the grand display,
Ms Von Teese wouldn't look.

Exiting the stage she caught the eye of a breakdancing pear,
who'd observed her failed audition and had a valid point to share.

"It's hard when you're not chosen," he said, practising his routine. "But this won't be the first or last time that you won't feel seen."

A bunch of grapes who'd just performed the can-can in a row,
delivered Dita wisdom as they saw her sadness grow.

"A peach isn't what they want right now,"
one said to Dita with care.

"But you'll be perfect for other parts,
there are plenty more out there!"

"You simply can't please everyone - no matter what you do - and changing yourself for others is an exhausting thing to do."

Dita held back tears as she met her mum outside. In fact, a giant part of her just wanted to run and hide.

But when she stopped and thought about all that the fruits had shared, she felt a little less miserable and less filled with despair.

"I may not be the ripest peach to Ms Von Teese, it's true.
But that's ok, I know that I am juicy to a few."

Her mother smiled from ear to ear as though Dita had wowed on stage, proud of the meaningful lesson she had learned at her tiny age.

"It won't always be easy when there's someone you can't reach. At times you will feel squashed and bruised when labelled 'just' a peach."

"But let's get one thing straight, you're more than juicy to a few.
Your talent lights up our family, our troupe is nothing without you."

Dita ballerina left that day without the part, but what she left the audition with had filled her little heart.

Ms Von Teese wasn't after a peach - she'd never change her mind - but not being someone's favourite doesn't mean that they're unkind.

It's okay for others to have different tastes and different points of view, because what we like and dislike is what makes me *me* and you *you*!

So be the best that you can be and celebrate being unique ...

... because what may not appeal to some

is exactly what others seek.

CPSIA information can be obtained
at www.ICGtesting.com
Printed in the USA
LVHW070024201220
674456LV00048B/117